Novels for Students, Volume 17

Project Editor: David Galens

Editorial: Anne Marie Hacht, Ira Mark Milne, Pam Revitzer, Kathy Sauer, Timothy J. Sisler, Jennifer Smith, Carol Ullmann, Maikue Vang

Research: Nicodemus Ford, Sarah Genik, Tamara Nott

Permissions: Shalice Shah-Caldwell

Manufacturing: Stacy Melson

Imaging and Multimedia: Dean Dauphinais, Leitha Etheridge-Sims, Mary Grimes, Lezlie Light, Luke Rademacher

Product Design: Pamela A. E. Galbreath, Michael Logusz

© 2003 by Gale. Gale is an imprint of The Gale group, Inc., a division of Thomson Learning Inc.

Gale and Design® and Thomson Learning™ are

trademarks used herein under license.

For more information, contact
The Gale Group, Inc.
27500 Drake Rd.
Farmington Hills, MI 48331–3535
Or you can visit our Internet site at
http://www.gale.com

ALL RIGHTS RESERVED
No part of this work covered by the copyright hereon may be reproduced or used in any form or by any means—graphic, electronic, or mechanical, including photocopying, recording, taping, Web distribution, or information storage retrieval systems—without the written permission of the publisher.

For permission to use material from this product, submit your request via Web at http://www.gale-edit.com/permissions, or you may download our Permissions Request form and submit your request by fax or mail to:

Permissions Department
The Gale Group, Inc.
27500 Drake Rd.
Farmington Hills, MI 48331-3535
Permissions Hotline: 248-699-8006 or 800-877-4253, ext. 8006
Fax: 248-699-8074 or 800-762-4058

Since this page cannot legibly accommodate all copyright notices, the acknowledgments constitute an extension of the copyright notice.

While every effort has been made to ensure the reliability of the information presented in this publication, The Gale Group, Inc. does not guarantee the accuracy of the data contained herein. The Gale Group, Inc. accepts no payment for listing; and inclusion in the publication of any organization, agency, institution, publication, service, or individual does not imply endorsement of the editors or publisher. Errors brought to the attention of the publisher and verified to the satisfaction of the publisher will be corrected in future editions.

ISBN 0-7876-6029-9
ISSN 1094-3552

Printed in the United States of America
10 9 8 7 6 5 4 3 2 1

The Big Sleep

Raymond Chandler 1939

Introduction

Raymond Chandler began writing his first novel, *The Big Sleep*, in 1938, and it was published in 1939. Critics consider it the best of the seven that he wrote. Before publishing the novel, Chandler wrote stories for pulp fiction magazines. He uses the plot and details from three of these stories, "Killer in the Rain," "The Curtain," and "Finger Man" in *The Big Sleep*. Alfred A. Knopf, Chandler's American publisher, promoted the book by linking Chandler with Dashiell Hammett and James M. Cain, two popular novelists of detective fiction also published by Knopf. Chandler's writing, however, was more hard-boiled than Cain or Hammett's. The narrator of the novel, private investigator Philip Marlowe, is a world-weary tough guy who nevertheless lives by a chivalric code of honor and retains a sense of professional pride in his work. He negotiates the decadent world of crime-ridden Los Angeles, trying to sort out the details of an increasingly complex scheme to blackmail the Sternwoods, a wealthy family that made its money in oil. The story is as much a character study of a certain male American mindset as it is a "whodunnit" crime story. More than simply a mystery novel, *The Big Sleep* has become a classic of American literature, with Chandler praised for his deft handling of plot, as well as his terse style and acerbic wit. Avon Books brought out the novel in paperback in 1943. In 1946, a film adaptation of *The Big Sleep* was released, starring Humphrey Bogart and Lauren Bacall, two of the biggest movie stars of the day.

Author Biography

Raymond Thornton Chandler was born July 23, 1888, in Chicago, Illinois, to Maurice Benjamin Chandler, a civil engineer, and Florence Thornton Chandler, a British immigrant. Chandlers' parents divorced when he was seven years old, he and his mother moved to London, England, to live with her family.

Chandler was educated at Dulwich College preparatory school, which taught students the value of public service and gentlemanly behavior as much as it did academic subjects such as mathematics and literature. After graduating from Dulwich, Chandler studied French in Paris, and spent time as a tutor in Germany before returning to England, where he worked as a civil servant for a brief period before growing disgusted with bureaucracy. In 1912, after trying and failing to make a living as a writer, Chandler moved back to the United States, where he worked at a variety of odd jobs until joining the Canadian army in 1917. Chandler saw limited time at the Western front in France during World War I and was training to be an air force pilot when the war ended. In 1924, Chandler married Pearl Cecily Eugenia Hurlburt, a woman twice-divorced and eighteen years his senior; the marriage lasted thirty years until her death in 1954. By the time of the marriage, Chandler had been employed for two years by Dabney Oil Syndicate in Los Angeles, rising through the ranks to become a vice president.

His affairs with office workers and his heavy drinking, however, led to his dismissal in 1932.

Chandler began writing stories for the pulp fiction market, publishing his work in outlets such as *Black Mask* and *Detective Fiction Weekly*, learning the trade as he went along. After years of what amounted to paid apprentice work writing for the pulps, Chandler published his first novel, *The Big Sleep* in 1939. It was a critical and popular success. Like Hammett, whose writing Chandler studied, Chandler set his stories in cities, and used the language of the streets. His meticulous attention to physical detail, complex plotting, and especially, his development of one of the greatest twentieth-century characters in American literature, private investigator Philip Marlowe, helped make Chandler one of the most popular mystery writers of his day. In Marlowe, Chandler created someone who, though exhausted and battered by the world's brutality and corruption, nonetheless lived by a code of honor and took pride in his work.

In addition to his short stories and seven novels, which include *Farewell, My Lovely* (1940) and *The Lady in the Lake* (1943), Chandler wrote screenplays for Hollywood including *Double Indemnity* (1944), *The Blue Dahlia* (1946), for which he received an Edgar Award from the Mystery Writers of America and an Oscar nomination for best screenplay, and *The Lady in the Lake* (1947). After a bout of pneumonia following a period of heavy drinking, Chandler died on March 26, 1959. He was, at the time, working on a new novel called *Poodle Springs*. The novel was later finished by Robert B. Parker and published in 1989.

Plot Summary

Chapters 1–5

The Big Sleep opens with private investigator Philip Marlowe visiting General Sternwood's mansion. Marlowe muses on the house's art and the fact that the furniture looks as if no one uses it. He first meets Carmen Sternwood, a flirt who, at twenty years old, is the younger of the General's two daughters. Then he meets the General, who receives him in his hothouse, a jungle-like setting in which the old man grows tropical orchids. The General tells Marlowe he is being blackmailed by someone named Arthur Gwynn Geiger, who wants the General to pay for Carmen's alleged gambling debts. Marlowe agrees to visit Geiger and put an end to the General's troubles. On his way out of the house, Vivian Regan, the older of the General's daughters, meets with Marlowe and tries to find out what the detective and her father spoke about, suspecting that it was about her husband, Rusty Regan, who left her about a month previously.

Pretending to be shopping for a rare book, Marlowe visits Geiger's antique bookstore, but Geiger is not in. While Marlowe waits for Geiger, a man comes in and disappears into a back room and then reappears with a book that he pays for and then leaves. Marlowe follows him a few blocks until the man hides the book in a tree. Marlowe, however, finds the book. Attempting to find Geiger, Marlowe visits another bookstore in the neighborhood and is given a description of Geiger by a woman who works there. He surmises through his discussion with this woman that Geiger's shop is a front for something. He discovers what that something is when he opens the book he had retrieved from the tree and sees that it contains pornographic photographs.

Chapters 6–10

Marlowe follows Geiger home and sees Carmen Sternwood's car parked in front of Geiger's home. He hears shots, and then breaks in to find Geiger dead on the floor and Carmen drugged and naked in front of a camera, the plateholder (negative) of which is missing. While rummaging through the house for clues, he finds a notebook with entries written in code. Marlowe takes Carmen home. The next morning, Bernie Ohls, the District Attorney's chief investigator, calls Marlowe and the two of them drive to the Lido fish pier where a man had driven into the ocean. The dead man is Owen Taylor, the Sternwoods' chauffeur, who once proposed to Carmen. Investigators cannot decide if the death was a homicide or a suicide. Marlowe returns to the city and visits Geiger's store once more, only to see men in the back room packing up books. He follows one of the men to Geiger's house, where the same man is packing up yet more books, and then to the apartment of Joe Brody.

Media Adaptations

- Warner Brothers released the film adaptation of Chandler's novel in 1946. The movie, directed by Howard Hawks, stars Humphrey Bogart and Lauren Bacall and is considered a classic of film noir. It is available in most libraries and video stores. Chandler's novel was adapted once more in 1978 in a film directed by Michael Winner and starring Robert Mitchum and Sarah Miles.

Chapters 11–16

Vivian Regan visits Marlowe and shows him a nude photograph of her sister taken at Geiger's house, claiming that someone is blackmailing her for $5,000 and will give the photo to the "scandal sheets" unless she pays up. She says that she can borrow the money from Eddie Mars, an owner of a gambling parlor that she frequents. Ohls tells Marlowe that all of the Sternwoods have alibis for last night. Hunting for more clues, Marlowe returns to Geiger's house, only to find Carmen Sternwood, who has gone there to retrieve the nude photographs taken of her. While Marlowe and Carmen are in the house, Eddie Mars arrives, telling Marlowe that Geiger is his tenant and threatening the private investigator with a gun. Marlowe heads to Joe Brody's apartment, and after a standoff that includes Agnes Lozelle, the blonde woman who works at Geiger's store and who is Brody's girlfriend, Marlowe learns that Brody was also at Geiger's the night Geiger was killed. Brody claims he saw Taylor running out of the house and he followed him, hit him on the head, and took the photographic plateholder Taylor himself had taken from Geiger's. Marlowe finally convinces him to give up the photographs and plateholder. Just then, Carmen knocks at the door, holding a gun to Brody and demanding the photographs. After a tussle, Brody gives the photos to Marlowe, and Carmen leaves. Shortly after she leaves, Carol Lundgren, the young man Marlowe had seen at Geiger's store, knocks on the door and shoots Brody dead when he answers. Marlowe chases him down and takes him back to Geiger's.

Chapters 17–19

Marlowe finds Geiger's body in a bed in

Lundgren's room and learns that Lundgren had been living with Geiger. Marlowe, Ohls, and Lundgren visit Taggart Wilde, the District Attorney, who is meeting with Captain Cronjager when they arrive. The two tell the story of the last few days but leave out a few details, specifically Carmen Sternwood's visit to Brody and Marlowe's run-in with Eddie Mars. The story goes as follows: Owen Taylor, who had once proposed to Carmen Sternwood, killed Geiger in a fit of rage when he found out Geiger was taking nude photographs of her. Brody tried to capitalize on the death by taking over Geiger's pornography business. Lundgren came home and moved Geiger's body to the back room, so that he would have time to move his things out of the house before the police found out about Geiger's murder. Lundgren sees Brody moving Geiger's pornographic books, and so believes that Brody killed Geiger. Lundgren kills Brody. Cronjager is upset because he is just learning about all of this the day after it happened. The next day, the newspapers report the Brody and Geiger murders solved, with Brody accused of killing Geiger over a shady business deal involving a wire service and Lundgren accused of killing Brody. The Sternwoods, Mars, Marlowe, and Ohls were not mentioned, nor did the papers connect the Taylor death to any of the events. Mars calls Marlowe to thank him for keeping his name out of his report.

Chapters 20–25

In these chapters, Marlowe hunts for Rusty

Regan, first visiting Captain Al Gregory of the Missing Persons Bureau, and then Eddie Mars's casino. Mars claims to know nothing. Marlowe "apparently" rescues Vivian Regan from a mugging outside the casino, and then takes her home. She attempts to seduce Marlowe, but he fends off her advances, asking her what information Mars has on her that she will not share with him. She says nothing. When Marlowe arrives home, he discovers Carmen in his bed and undressed. Again, Marlowe declines an invitation for sex and kicks Carmen out. The next day, Harry Jones, a two-bit grifter who had been tailing Marlowe, tells him that Eddie Mars had Regan killed and that Mona Grant, Eddie's estranged wife, is hiding out outside of town.

Chapters 26–32

Marlowe visits Puss Walgreen's insurance offices and overhears Jones talking to Lash Canino. He listens as Jones tells Canino where Lozelle is hiding out and then listens as Canino poisons Jones by pouring him a cyanide-laced drink. Marlowe calls Lozelle and offers her two hundred dollars for information about Mona Grant's whereabouts. After paying her and receiving the information, Marlowe heads out of town, where he runs into Canino and Art Huck, who runs an auto repair garage. The two beat up Marlowe and handcuff him. He wakes up to see Grant in a silver wig guarding him. After Marlowe tells her that Mars is a killer, she lets him escape. Marlowe waits outside for Canino to return and then, with Grant creating a diversion, shoots

Canino dead. The next day Marlowe visits General Sternwood and explains to him why he kept looking for Regan even after the General had told him the case was closed. The General first feigns anger and then offers Marlowe a thousand dollars to find Regan. On his way out of the house, Marlowe sees Carmen and she asks him to teach her how to shoot a gun. She takes Marlowe down an old deserted road and, during target practice, shoots at him, but does not kill him because he had loaded the gun with blanks. Carmen has an epileptic seizure and Marlowe takes her home. He tells Vivian what happened and finally discovers the truth from her: Carmen had killed Regan because he refused her advances. With Eddie Mars's help, they disposed of the body in an old oil well. Marlowe makes Vivian promise to take Carmen away and get professional help for her, threatening to report the details of Regan's murder if she does not. She agrees and Marlowe leaves, musing on death and how nothing matters when one is doing "the big sleep."

Characters

Joe Brody

Joe Brody is a small-time hood who was once involved with Carmen Sternwood; her father paid him to stop seeing his daughter. Brody's new girlfriend is Agnes, Geiger's employee. Brody has successfully blackmailed the General once and tries to do it again with nude photos of Carmen, which he took off Taylor after following Taylor from Geiger's home. Lundgren kills Brody because he believed that Brody had killed his lover, Geiger.

Lash Canino

Lash Canino is a cold and ruthless hit man who wears brown clothes and a brown hat and drives a brown car. He works for Mars as a bodyguard and all purpose thug. Canino helps to dispose of Rusty Regan's body after Carmen Sternwood kills him. He also poisons Jones after extracting information from him about Agnes's location. Marlowe kills Canino in a shoot-out.

Larry Cobb

Larry Cobb is a drunk and Vivian Regan's escort at the Cypress Club.

Captain Cronjager

Captain Cronjager, "a hatchet-faced man," is at Wilde's home when Marlowe and Ohls chronicle the events leading up to and including Geiger and Brody's murders. He is angry with Marlowe for not reporting the murders earlier and the two of them argue.

Arthur Gwynn Geiger

Arthur Gwynn Geiger is a pornographer who owns a rare book store on Hollywood Boulevard and rents a house from Mars. A middle-aged "fattish" man with a Charlie Chan moustache, Geiger is shot dead while taking photographs of a nude Carmen Sternwood. His lover is Lundgren, who also lives in the house.

Mona Grant

Mona Grant is a former lounge singer and Mars's estranged wife. She is also a former girlfriend of Rusty Regan. She is hiding outside of town and guarded by Canino, so that the police will think that she ran away with Regan. Initially, she is naive and gullible, refusing to believe Marlowe when he tells her that Mars kills people, but she lets Marlowe escape while she is guarding him, and then helps him kill Canino by creating a diversion.

Captain Al Gregory

Al Gregory is head of the Missing Persons Bureau. Marlowe describes him as "a burly man with tired eyes." He knows more than he lets on, initially presenting himself as a "hack," but later telling Marlowe that he is an honest man in a dishonest city. Gregory shows Marlowe a photograph of Regan and provides him with information about his history.

Art Huck

Art Huck, a gaunt man in overalls, owns a house and an auto repair shop outside of the city. He and Canino are protecting Grant, who is hiding out at Huck's place. Huck fixes Marlowe's flats and then helps Canino capture him.

Harry Jones

Harry Jones is a small-time criminal and friend of Brody and Rusty Regan's. He tells Marlowe that Mars had Regan killed. He is a small man with bright eyes. He sums up his philosophy of life when he tells Marlowe, "I'm a grifter. We're all grifters. So we sell each other out for a nickel." He is poisoned by Canino, after Jones tells the killer where Agnes is hiding.

Agnes Lozelle

Agnes Lozelle is Joe Brody's ash-blonde girl-friend who works in Geiger's store. She is surly and aloof when Marlowe visits the store, arousing his suspicions. She bemoans her luck at always attracting "half-smart" men. After Brody is killed, she connects with Jones, who tries to protect her from Canino. Marlowe gives her two hundred dollars for information about Mona Grant.

Carol Lundgren

Carol Lundgren worked for Geiger, was his lover, and lived with him. He is a good-looking, thin, blonde young man who Marlowe refers to as a "fag" and a "pansy." After Lundgren shoots Brody, Marlowe chases him down and brings him back to Geiger's house. He is arrested and charged with Brody's murder.

Philip Marlowe

Philip Marlowe, the novel's narrator, is a single, thirty-three year old private investigator. Marlowe had formerly worked for Wilde, the District Attorney, but was fired for insubordination. He is a handsome, charming, cynical, street-smart character who loves his work but shows contempt for women. When he is not smoking or drinking, he is nursing a hangover and working the Sternwood case. Marlowe has a high degree of professional pride and a general disdain for the rich. He puts work before romance and is loyal to his employer, General Sternwood, declining the amorous advances of both of Sternwood's daughters. Arrogant, witty, self-deprecating, and world-weary, Marlowe served and continues to serve as the inspiration for the characters of numerous private investigators in both fiction and film.

Eddie Mars

Eddie Mars is the middle-aged proprietor of the Cypress Club, a gambling house on the beach that Vivian Regan frequents. He also rents a house to Geiger. Impeccably dressed in expensive gray suits, Mars has a cool demeanor and rarely involves himself directly in crime, choosing instead to hire others such as Canino to do his dirty work. His wife, Grant, was once Rusty Regan's lover. Mars has connections in the police department and it is likely that he will not be charged with any crimes.

Mathilda

Mathilda is Vivian Regan's maid. Marlowe describes her as "a middle-aged woman with a long gentle face."

Vincent Norris

Vincent Norris is General Sternwood's butler. He is about sixty years old, with silver hair, an agile manner, and a quick wit. He holds a considerable degree of power in the Sternwood household, writing checks for the General and deciding what information the General should and should not have.

Bernie Ohls

Bernie Ohls is the chief investigator for Wilde and a friend of Marlowe's who had recommended Marlowe to General Sternwood. Ohls is tough, having killed nine men during his career. But he also takes pride in his work and has a degree of integrity. He takes Marlowe to see Owen Taylor's body and accompanies him to Wilde's to report the details of Brody and Geiger's murder and subsequently to report Jones's and Canino's deaths.

Terence Regan

Terence "Rusty" Regan is an Irish immigrant, former bootlegger, and late husband of Vivian Regan. Regan was a good friend of General Sternwood, who would listen to his stories of the time he spent in the Irish Republican Army. He was in love with Grant, Mars's wife, and becomes the object of Marlowe's investigation in the second half of the novel, after General Sternwood hires Marlowe to find him. Regan is killed by Carmen Sternwood after he spurns her advances.

Vivian Regan

The oldest Sternwood daughter, Vivian is in her 20s and almost as hard-boiled as Marlowe, spending most of her time at the roulette table at the Cypress Club gambling or drinking and attempting to seduce men like Marlowe, who describes her as "tall and rangy and strong-looking." Her escort is

Larry Cobb, a slobbering drunk for whom she has no affection but considered marrying at one point. She has been married three times, most recently to Rusty Regan. She helps to cover up the truth of Regan's death by deceiving Marlowe to protect her sister. She finally tells Marlowe the details of his death at the end of the novel.

Carmen Sternwood

Carmen Sternwood is the younger of the two Sternwood sisters. She is twenty years old, beautiful, relentlessly flirtatious, spoiled, and epileptic. She is also at the center of the blackmailing scheme that includes Geiger and Brody. She spends most of the novel sucking on her thumb or playing with her hair, or telling Marlowe that he is cute. After being sexually rejected by Marlowe a number of times, she attempts to shoot him while Marlowe is showing her how to use a gun. Her sister tells Marlowe that Carmen had killed Regan for the same reason. Marlowe makes Vivian promise to seek professional help for her sister as a condition for him to remain silent about the details of Regan's death.

General Gus Sternwood

General Sternwood is the elderly millionaire father of Carmen and Vivian, who initially hires Marlowe to "take care" of someone who is attempting to blackmail him. He fell off a horse when he was fifty-eight years old and is paralyzed from the waist down. Sternwood now lives through others, spending most of his time in a wheelchair in his hothouse growing orchids. He loved Rusty Regan because Regan told him stories and kept him company, and he hires Marlowe to find him. Norris and the daughters keep the truth of Regan's death from him.

Owen Taylor

Taylor was "a slim dark-haired kid" from Dubuque, Iowa who worked as a chauffeur for the Sternwoods. His body is found in a car off the Lido pier and his death is ruled a suicide. Marlowe speculates that Taylor killed Geiger when he found out he was taking nude photographs of Carmen Sternwood, to whom Taylor had once proposed.

Taggart Wilde

Taggart Wilde is the District Attorney and Marlowe's former boss. He comes from an old Los Angeles family and his political connections are many and deep. His father was a friend of General Sternwood's. Marlowe describes him as "a middle-aged plump man with clear blue eyes that managed to have a friendly expression without really having any expression at all." He determines what will be reported in the newspapers regarding Brody and Geiger's killings and helps keep the Sternwood name out of the papers.

Themes

Privilege and Entitlement

Although Marlowe works for General Sternwood, a millionaire, his loyalty to the man is not based on Sternwood's wealth but on his age, infirmity, and honesty. Throughout the novel, Marlowe treats people as they treat him, rather than as they expect to be treated by virtue of their class standing or social position. This is demonstrated in the way he responds to the Sternwood sisters, both of whom are privileged and behave as if they are entitled to special treatment. Vivian Regan is shocked by Marlowe's "rude manners" during their first encounter, and Carmen Sternwood is so disturbed by Marlowe's sexual rejection of her that she attempts to kill him. Marlowe is also discourteous to Captain Cronjager during his visit to Wilde's office, refusing to defer to Cronjager's position as police captain when discussing the Geiger and Brody killings. Marlowe's behavior in this instance has as much to do with his own sense of entitlement regarding what he can and cannot do in his job as a private investigator as it does with Cronjager's arrogance.

Meaning of Life

In the early twentieth century, the sheer horror and scale of atrocities during the first World War caused many people to lose faith in God and organized religion. Combined with the increasing acceptance of scientific theories such as evolution, many no longer believed in a higher benevolent intelligence to provide meaning to their lives, and so, struggled to find purpose. Some, like the Sternwood sisters, spent their time pursuing pleasure gambling, drinking, and engaging in promiscuous sex. Others, like Marlowe, found meaning in their work and in adherence to a code of honor. Still others, such as General Sternwood, who had lost control of much of his body, survived by living through people like Marlowe and Rusty Regan. Death, however, hovers just above the heads of all the characters, as Marlowe reminds readers at the end of the novel: "What did it matter where you lay once you were dead? ... You just slept the big sleep, not caring about the nastiness of how you died or where you fell."

Topics for Further Study

- Divide the class into four groups and assign each group eight chapters from the novel. Each group should compile a list of terms from their respective chapters that Marlowe and other characters use that are peculiar to the detective-story genre. Such terms might include words like "gat" (gun) or "peeper" (private investigator). Compile all of the terms into a dictionary for the class.

- Watch the 1946 film adaptation of Chandler's novel and list the differences between the film and the novel. Discuss possible reasons for those differences as a class.

- Rewrite the last chapter in the book, resolving the Rusty Regan mystery in a different way. Exchange your chapter with a classmate and discuss in pairs.

- While screenwriters were working on adapting Chandler's novel to film, they sent him a note asking how Owen Taylor really died. Chandler responded, saying he did not know. On the board, brainstorm possible theories of Taylor's death and vote as a class on the best theory.

- In pairs, make a list of your favorite similes in the novel and then put them on the board and as a class discuss what makes them effective.

Law and Order

Laws are meant to ensure a safe environment for citizens, to maintain social order, and to instill a sense of justice in the populace. The rampant corruption and disregard for the law in Chandler's novel demonstrates that the social fabric has begun to fray in 1930s Los Angeles. Police protect pornographers and gamblers, women destroy men for sport, the wealthy buy their way out of trouble, and appearances inevitably belie reality. Characters routinely manipulate each other for personal gain. The spirit of Chandler's novel can be summed up by small-time criminal Harry Jones, who says to Marlowe, "We're all grifters. So we sell each other out for a nickel."

Style

Dialogue

Dialogue, the conversation between two or more characters, is a primary tool writers use for characterization and to drive plots. Writers use dialogue to reveal the desires, motivations, and character of the players in their stories, helping to create an idea and an image of them in readers' minds. Chandler is known as a master of vernacular dialogue. His characters talk the way that 1930s thugs, cops, and private investigators talk on the job, in language studded with slang such as "loogan" (a man with a gun), "peeper" (private investigator), and "centuries" (hundred dollar bills). His characters, especially Marlowe, are also known for their use of biting similes to describe someone or thing. Similes are comparisons that employ "as" or "like." For example, in describing the way Brody's cigarette dangles from his mouth, Marlowe states: "His cigarette was jiggling like a doll on a coiled spring." This is also an example of Marlowe's wit, which he uses to ward off sentimentality and to demonstrate his self-awareness.

Description

The bulk of Chandler's novel is objective description. Marlowe spends a long time describing the physical settings of individual scenes, thus making a kind of character out of place. This strategy creates vivid images in readers' minds, helps to develop characterization, and prepares readers for the ensuing action. Marlowe's elaborate description of Geiger's house as a virtual palace of tackiness, for example, emphasizes Geiger's sordid behavior as a pornographer and (to Marlowe) as a homosexual. Chandler was heavily influenced by Ernest Hemingway's use of description in his novels of the 1920s.

Plot

Plot refers to the arrangement of events in a story. In Chandler's novel, details of the events come fast. However, the interpretation of the events change as Marlowe receives new information, causing readers to rethink what they believe as well. For example, at first Ohls and Marlowe believe that Taylor had committed suicide. However, when they discover a bruise on his forehead, they believe he was hit by a blackjack and murdered. Later however, Brody claims to have hit Taylor but not to have killed him with the blow. The truth of what actually happened to Taylor is never revealed. Unlike conventional mystery novels where all loose ends are tied up, *The Big Sleep* leaves many questions unanswered and plot details unresolved.

Historical Context

1930s

While Chandler was penning his novel in the late 1930s, the United States was attempting to recover from the depression that had economically devastated the country since 1929. Marlowe, who charged millionaire General Sternwood twenty-five dollars a day plus expenses, was not only working, he was making well over the average national salary, which stood at $1,368. Unemployment during the 1930s reached a high of 25%. To help alleviate the economic suffering of many Americans, President Roosevelt signed the Social Security Act and the Wagner Act in 1935, ensuring the elderly an income, and ensuring workers the right to unionize, respectively.

Farmers were especially hard hit during the 1930s, and many from Midwestern "Dust Bowl" states such as Oklahoma and Missouri (so named because of the drought and dust storms that hit that area in the 1930s) moved to California hoping for work and a better life. On the outskirts of Marlowe's Los Angeles and in the fertile valleys of the state, migrant workers picked lemons, potatoes, cotton, peas, and other crops, going wherever there was work. The Works Progress Administration, a huge government job program, was also created in 1935. Over its seven-year life span the WPA spent eleven billion dollars employing more than eight million people for 250,000 projects that involved rebuilding the country's roads, bridges, and public buildings. The WPA also provided work for artists, writers, and musicians, as the federal government broadly sponsored the arts for the first time.

Sternwood, who made his millions in oil, would have been interested in the Public Utility Holding Company Act of 1935. The Act created a new federal agency, the Federal Power Commission, which regulated electricity prices, while the Federal Trade Commission did the same for natural gas prices. Many business people fought against components of Roosevelt's New Deal, claiming that they hindered job creation and development of markets, but Roosevelt remained resolute.

The literature of the 1930s explored issues of integrity and honor. Ernest Hemingway's novels, *To Have and Have Not* (1937) and *For Whom the Bell Tolls* (1939), for example, both featured characters who pitted themselves against larger forces such as corporations and fascism. John Steinbeck's *Grapes of Wrath* (1939) chronicled the struggles of the Joad family, tenant farmers crippled by the depression and the effects of corporate capitalism. Hollywood, on the other hand, where Chandler would make his mark during the 1940s writing screenplays, offered less weighty fare, providing escapist entertainment for the masses. Films popular during this time include *Topper* (1937), *Bringing Up Baby* (1938), and Frank Capra's *Mr. Smith Goes to Washington*

(1939). Film noir, elements of which Chandler helped to define in his novels and screenplays, was just beginning to take shape in movies such as *The Maltese Falcon* (1941), featuring Humphrey Bogart playing Hammett's Sam Spade, and *This Gun for Hire* (1942). The 1940s, of course, was noir's heyday, with Chandler writing the screenplays for classics such as *Double Indemnity* (1944) and *The Blue Dahlia* (1946), and seeing his novels *Farewell My Lovely*, *The Big Sleep*, and *The Lady in the Lake* adapted for the big screen.

Critical Overview

Knopf published *The Big Sleep* in America in 1939 and Hamish Hamilton published the first English edition the same year. The novel received brief but favorable reviews in publications in both countries, with reviewers likening Chandler's work to that of Dashiell Hammett's, the foremost writer of detective novels in the 1920s and 1930s. The first American printing of 5,000 copies sold out quickly, and a second printing was ordered immediately in both the United States and England. Chandler's publishers were so pleased with his success they offered him a 20 percent royalty for the first 5,000 copies of his next novel, and 25 percent on any copies sold beyond that.

Compare & Contrast

- **1930s:** The economy of the United States continues to slump after a massive downturn in the stock market, which began in 1929 and led to the Great Depression.

  Today: After a massive boom, the economy of the United States slumps after a massive downturn in the stock market, which began in 2000.

- **1930s:** To combat widespread crime

in the United States various federal government agencies within the Department of Justice are consolidated to form the Federal Bureau of Investigation.

Today: After the attacks on the World Trade Center and the Pentagon, President Bush forms the Office of Homeland Security to strengthen protection against terrorist threats and attacks in the United States.

- **1930s:** Although gambling is illegal, many gambling houses exist, and often have police protection.

  Today: State lotteries are commonplace and many states have legal gambling casinos, many of them operating on Native-American reservations.

After Chandler's death, his reputation as a serious writer grew, with many critics claiming *The Big Sleep* as his best novel. In his biography, *The Life of Raymond Chandler*, Frank MacShane argues that although the novel was in reality a stitching together and elaboration of three short stories, the completed product was more than the sum of its parts. MacShane writes, "It is as if the creation of the original images required the sort of emotional energy that makes a poet remember his lines years after he first wrote them down." Other critics consider Chandler's use of Marlowe as the first-person narrator the key ingredient in the novel's success. Russell Davies, for example, in his essay, "Omnes Me Impune Lacessunt," claims Marlowe's self-mockery and "the balance of ironies" in the novel "is really the secret of Chandler's success."

Critic Clive James agrees, noting, "In *The Big Sleep* and all the novels that followed, the secret of plausibility lies in the style, and the secret of the style lies in Marlowe's personality." Jerry Speir also focuses on Marlowe in discussing the novel. However, instead of treating Marlowe as a knight-errant as have many other critics, Speir argues, "*The Big Sleep* might be read as a *failure* of romance." Daniel Linder draws attention to the linguistic irony in the novel in his essay for *The Explicator*, arguing that Carmen Sternwood's repeated use of the words "cute" and "giggle" have an "echoic" effect on readers that demands interpretation.

What Do I Read Next?

- Another popular Chandler novel chronicling the adventures of Phillip Marlowe is *The Long Goodbye*, published in 1953. This novel was made into a Hollywood film (1973) directed by Robert Altman and starring Elliot Gould.

- Al Clark's *Raymond Chandler in Hollywood* (1982) explores Chandler's life when he was writing screenplays for films such as *Double Indemnity* and *The Blue Dahlia*.

- In 1994, Robert Parker, considered by many to be Chandler's successor as king of the hardboiled detective novel, wrote *Perchance to Dream*, a sequel to *The Big Sleep*. Parker also finished the novel Chandler was working on when he died: *Poodle Springs* (1986).

- Edward Thorpe's *Chandlertown: The Los Angeles of Philip Marlowe* (1983) examines the role Los Angeles plays in Chandler's detective fiction.

Sources

Chandler, Raymond, *The Big Sleep*, Vintage, 1992, pp. 114, 204.

——, "The Simple Art of Murder," in *Atlantic Monthly*, December 1944, p. 59.

Davies, Russell, "Omnes Me Impune Lacessunt," in *The World of Raymond Chandler*, edited by Miriam Gross, Weidenfeld and Nicolson, 1977, pp. 32–42.

James, Clive, "The Country behind the Hill," in *The World of Raymond Chandler*, edited by Miriam Gross, Weidenfeld and Nicolson, 1977, pp. 116–26.

Linder, Daniel, "The Big Sleep," in the *Explicator*, Vol. 59, Issue 3, Spring 2001, p. 137.

MacShane, Frank, *The Life of Raymond Chandler*, Hammish Hamilton Ltd., 1986, p. 68.

Speir, Jerry, *Raymond Chandler*, Frederick Ungar Publishing, 1981, p. 30.

Further Reading

Durham, Philip, *Down These Mean Streets a Man Must Go: Raymond Chandler's Knight*, University of North Carolina Press, 1963.

> Durham examines Marlowe's code of chivalric behavior in this ingenious study.

Hiney, Tom, *Raymond Chandler: A Biography*, Atlantic Monthly Press, 1997.

> Hiney draws on Chandler's papers and letters to construct this engaging biography.

Marling, William, *Raymond Chandler*, Twayne, 1986.

> Marling provides a solid and accessible introduction to Chandler's fiction in this study.

Van Dover, J. K., ed., *The Critical Responses to Raymond Chandler*, Greenwood, 1995.

> This collection of essays covers a wide range of critical approaches to Chandler's novels.